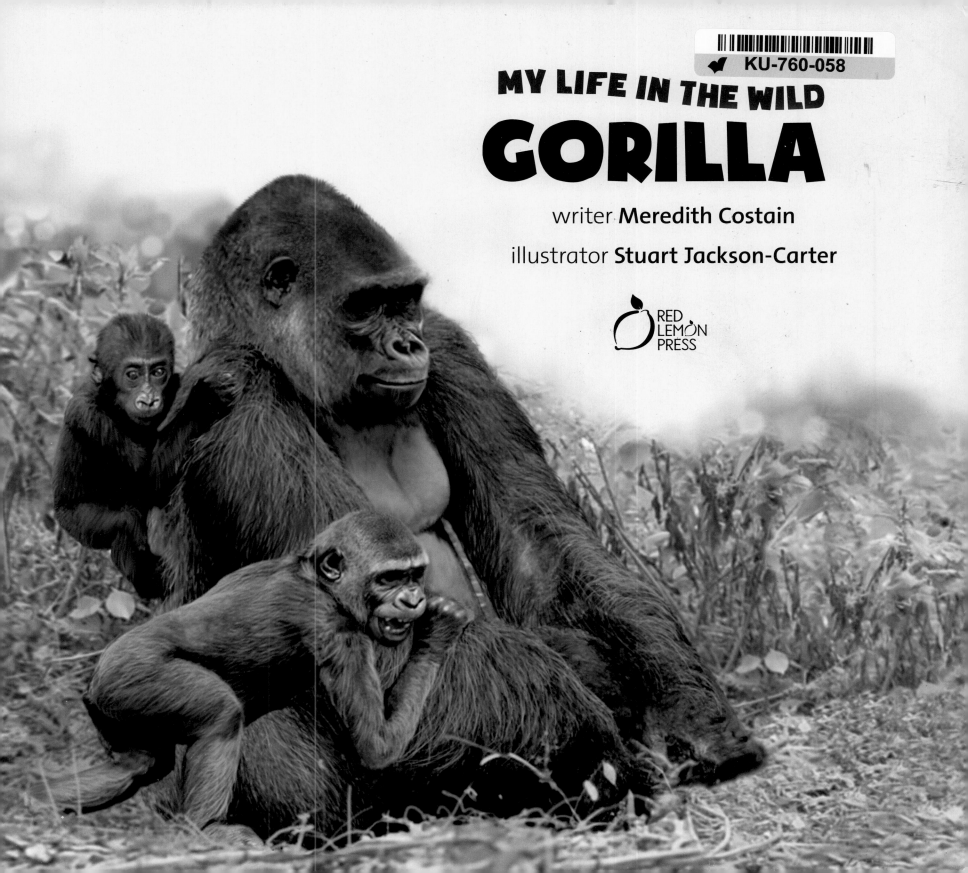

MY LIFE IN THE WILD
GORILLA

writer **Meredith Costain**

illustrator **Stuart Jackson-Carter**

RED
LEMON
PRESS

I am a western lowland gorilla.
I am tall and strong, with long arms and black hair. My home is the rainforest of central Africa. People think I look fierce, but I'm really very gentle. Let me tell you my story.

I am born late at night. Mum licks me clean, then holds me against her chest. I cling to her soft fur. I nuzzle around until I find her milk, then begin to drink.

The next morning, the rest of my troop gathers around to meet me. Mum holds me tightly in her strong arms. Dad looks on proudly. I blink sleepily at my new family.

Each morning, we set off to a new area of the rainforest, searching for food to eat. Dad leads the way.

I'm old enough now to ride on my mother's back.
I can see the whole forest from up here!

Dad finds us a place full of juicy plants.
We settle down on the forest floor to eat.
Mum finds me a tasty shoot to munch on.
We keep eating until our bellies are full.

After our meal we settle down to rest. Mum pulls together some plants and branches to make our nest. Then she rakes her long fingers gently through my fur until I fall asleep.

Every day I grow bigger and stronger. Life in our troop is fun. I play with my friends, tumbling, wrestling, climbing trees and play-fighting.

My friend pulls my ear. I put him in a headlock, making him screech. I screech back and we go tumbling through the bushes, hooting and hollering. The others cheer us on.

Suddenly, everything goes quiet. Dad is standing over us, glaring. We're making too much noise. We bow our heads and scamper back to the safety of our mothers' laps.

Another silverback comes snooping around. Maybe he'll try to take my mother away!

Roaring and rumbling, my dad rears up and beats his chest to show who's boss. Then he tears up plants and thumps the ground. The silverback slinks away.

Time passes. I am now much bigger than my mother. I have two little sisters to play with, and many new cousins.

Our troop is growing all the time. It will soon be time to leave my family and start my own.

My days of carefree play are long gone.
I now have a family of my own to protect
and care for.

I lead the way through the rainforest, searching for a good place to eat, as my father did before me.

Did You Know?

Baby gorillas are usually born at night.

Female gorillas give birth to a single infant about every four years. The baby is very small – about half the weight of a human newborn. The mother holds the baby close to her belly until it is strong enough to cling to her fur.

Gorillas are curious about new family members.

When a new infant is born, the rest of the troop is eager to meet it. At first, the mother gorilla is very protective of her baby. She lovingly cradles it in her arms. After a short while, she allows the other gorillas to look at and touch their new family member.

Gorillas move about in different ways.

For the first three months, a gorilla baby clings to its mother's chest when she sits or travels. Older infants ride on their mother's back. By three years of age, they are strong enough to walk by themselves over long distances. Gorillas 'knucklewalk' on all fours when moving around.

Gorillas need to eat large amounts of food.

Gorillas eat leaves, stems, bark, shoots, buds and berries. If very hungry, they might also eat insects, slugs and snails. Their body is so large they need to spend six or seven hours a day eating. Adult male gorillas need to eat as much as 18 kilograms (40 lbs) of food a day.

Gorillas build two new nests each day.

During the day, gorillas pull branches and plants together to make a simple nest on the ground to rest in. Mothers often use this time to bond with and groom their offspring, combing their fur with their fingers and teeth to remove dirt and insects. At night they build a nest either in the fork of a tree or on the ground to sleep in.

Play is very important to young gorillas.

Climbing, wrestling and play-fighting allow gorillas to test their strength and to learn survival skills. A rainforest provides a giant adventure playground for them to explore and play in.

Did You Know? (continued)

Gorillas make a variety of sounds.

Gorillas make many different sounds, including barking, screaming, belching, grunting and hooting. Just like humans, they also sneeze, cough, yawn, hiccup, burp and laugh. The call of a silverback can be heard up to 8 kilometres (5 m) away.

The silverback is the leader of the group and the centre of family life.

The silverback makes all the decisions about where to feed or where to stop for the night. The father of all the young gorillas in the troop, he keeps an eye on the youngsters from the time they are born to when they are 'teens', making sure their games don't become too rowdy.

Silverbacks scare away intruders.

If another adult male approaches his group, the silverback will put on a display that shows off how strong he is to scare him away. He beats his chest with his cupped hands, hoots and roars, tears up plants and snaps branches. Finally, he dashes toward the intruder and thumps the ground in front of him.

Male gorillas eventually leave to form new family groups.

Between the ages of 8 and 12, male gorillas are known as blackbacks. At around 11, the males slowly begin to leave their troop. They travel alone or with a small group of other males for a few years before they form a new troop of their own.

The habitat of gorillas is shrinking.

A gorilla's home range is normally about 13 square kilometres (5 m²). However, as more and more of their habitat is destroyed by people, they need to extend their range to be able to find enough food to survive.

Meet the Primate Family

Gorillas belong to a group of mammals known as primates. Here are some other members of the primate family:

Orangutan

Chimpanzee

Lar gibbon

QUIZ

1. How many different types of primates can you see here?

2. Which primate looks the most like the western lowland gorilla?

3. Which primate has the longest arms?

4. How many of these primates have tails?

Western lowland gorilla

Scientific name: *Gorilla gorilla gorilla*

Coat colour: Black to brownish grey. Mature males have a silver-grey saddle across their back and upper thighs.

Height: 1.3–1.9 metres (4¼–6¼ ft)

Weight: 68–200 kilograms (150–430 lbs)

Weight at birth: 1.4–1.8 kg (3–4 lbs)

Habitat: Tropical rainforests of west central Africa

Number of teeth: 32, in two sets (the same as humans)

Life span: 35 years

Conservation status: Endangered

Where gorillas live

AFRICA

Western lowland gorilla

Ring-tailed lemur

Baboon

Woolly monkey

6. Which of these primates is the largest?

8. Which primates have long shaggy fur?

5. Which primate has a stripy tail and a masked face?

7. Which primate has a long snout?

Glossary

blink	to open and close eyes quickly
carefree	having no worries or problems
holler	to yell, shout
nuzzle	to touch, push or rub the nose against
protect	to keep safe
rainforest	a thick, tropical forest that receives a lot of rain
rake	to comb
scamper	to run quickly and playfully
shoot	new plant growth
silverback	a mature male gorilla with silver hair on his back
troop	a family of gorillas

RED LEMON PRESS

Published in the UK by:
Red Lemon Press (an imprint of Weldon Owen)
Deepdene Lodge,
Deepdene Avenue,
Dorking,
Surrey RH5 4AT
www.weldonowen.co.uk

Conceived and produced by
Weldon Owen Pty Ltd
Ground Floor 42—44 Victoria Street, McMahons Point
Sydney NSW 2060, Australia
weldonowenpublishing.com

Copyright © 2012 Weldon Owen Pty Ltd

WELDON OWEN PTY LTD
Managing Director Kay Scarlett
Publisher Corinne Roberts
Creative Director Sue Burk
**Senior Vice President,
International Sales** Stuart Laurence
Sales Manager, North America Ellen Towell
**Administration Manager,
International Sales** Kristine Ravn

Managing Editor Helen Bateman
Consultant Professor Phil Whitfield
Design Concept Cooling Brown Ltd
Designer Gabrielle Green
Images Manager Trucie Henderson
Production Director Todd Rechner
Production and Prepress Controller Mike Crowton
Illustrations Stuart Jackson-Carter/KJA-artists
except Meet the Primate Family pages.

ISBN: 978-1-78342-144-2

Printed and bound in China.

A WELDON OWEN PRODUCTION